Optimism

I0620196

Transform Your Life with Unshakable Confidence: The
Power of Optimism - Your Ultimate Guide to Finding Joy,
Overcoming Adversity and Achieving Success

Lance P. Richards

Optimism: Transform Your Life with Unshakable Confidence: The Power of Optimism - Your Ultimate Guide to Finding Joy, Overcoming Adversity and Achieving Success

Table of Contents

01: Introduction: Understanding the Power of Optimism

The power of optimism is often overlooked, yet it has the potential to transform your life in profound ways. It has the power to help you overcome adversity, find joy in the present moment, and achieve success in all areas of your life. The foundation of optimism lies in the way you think and view the world. An optimistic outlook can bring a sense of hope and positivity to your life, making it easier to navigate through life's challenges and find joy in everyday experiences.

Optimism is not just a fleeting feeling or a temporary state of mind. It is a mindset that you can cultivate and strengthen over time. This guide is designed to help you understand the power of optimism and how it can transform your life. You'll learn about the science behind optimism, the benefits of an optimistic outlook, and practical strategies for cultivating a positive mindset.

The Science Behind Optimism

The study of optimism has been a topic of interest for scientists for many years. Research has shown that optimism

01: INTRODUCTION: UNDERSTANDING THE POWER OF OPTIMISM

is linked to better physical health, increased happiness and life satisfaction, and improved coping skills during times of stress and adversity. In fact, people who are optimistic are more likely to engage in healthy behaviors, have stronger relationships, and experience less stress and anxiety.

Optimism can be described as a cognitive bias that tends to emphasize positive outcomes and downplay negative outcomes. It is a way of thinking that sees the glass as half full, rather than half empty. This type of thinking can help to reduce stress, increase resilience, and boost overall well-being.

The Benefits of an Optimistic Outlook

The benefits of optimism are numerous and far-reaching. People who are optimistic tend to experience less stress, anxiety, and depression. They also tend to have more energy and a more positive outlook on life, which can help them to achieve their goals and live a more fulfilling life.

Optimism can also have a significant impact on your physical health. Research has shown that people who are optimistic tend to have lower levels of inflammation, which is a risk factor for many chronic health conditions. They are also less likely to develop chronic health problems such as heart disease, diabetes, and certain types of cancer.

Another benefit of optimism is that it can improve your relationships. People who are optimistic tend to have better relationships with their friends, family, and coworkers. They are seen as more likable and are more likely to be sought after as friends and allies. This is because optimism is contagious, and people are naturally drawn to those who have a positive outlook on life.

In addition, optimism can help you achieve your goals and live a more successful life. People who are optimistic are more likely to take action towards their goals, persevere in the face of adversity, and bounce back from setbacks. This is because they have a sense of hope and believe that things will work out in the end.

In conclusion, the power of optimism should not be underestimated. It has the potential to transform your life in profound ways, helping you to find joy, overcome adversity, and achieve success. This guide will provide you with the tools and strategies you need to cultivate an optimistic out-

01: INTRODUCTION: UNDERSTANDING THE POWER OF OPTIMISM

look and tap into the power of optimism to live a happier, healthier, and more fulfilling life.

02: The Science Behind Optimism: How It Impacts Your Life

Optimism is a powerful force that can have a profound impact on your life. It has been the subject of numerous scientific studies and has been found to be linked to a wide range of physical and mental health benefits. The science behind optimism reveals that it is much more than just a positive attitude or a sunny disposition. Rather, it is a cognitive bias that influences the way you perceive and respond to the world around you.

One of the key ways that optimism impacts your life is by reducing stress and anxiety. When you approach life with an optimistic outlook, you are less likely to worry about the future and more likely to focus on the present moment. This can help to reduce stress levels and improve overall mental health.

Studies have also shown that optimism can improve physical health. People who are optimistic tend to have lower levels of inflammation, which is a risk factor for many chronic health conditions, such as heart disease and diabetes. Additionally, they are less likely to develop chronic health problems, such as cardiovascular disease, cancer, and other serious health conditions.

The benefits of optimism extend to your relationships as well. People who are optimistic tend to have stronger relationships with friends, family, and coworkers. They are more likable and are often sought after as friends and allies. This is because optimism is contagious, and people are naturally drawn to those with a positive outlook on life.

Another way that optimism can impact your life is by helping you achieve your goals. When you approach life with a positive outlook, you are more likely to take action towards your goals, persevere in the face of adversity, and bounce back from setbacks. This is because you have a sense of hope and believe that things will work out in the end.

It is important to note that the science behind optimism is still in its early stages, and much more research is needed to fully understand its impact on our lives. However, the available evidence suggests that optimism can have a profound impact on your health, relationships, and overall well-being.

In conclusion, the science behind optimism provides compelling evidence of its ability to positively impact your life.

02: THE SCIENCE BEHIND OPTIMISM: HOW IT IMPACTS YOUR LIFE

By cultivating an optimistic outlook, you can reduce stress and anxiety, improve physical and mental health, strengthen relationships, and achieve your goals. Whether you are facing a difficult challenge or simply looking to live a happier, healthier life, optimism can be a powerful tool for transformation.

03: The Benefits of an Optimistic Outlook

An optimistic outlook on life can have a profound impact on your happiness, health, and success. This positive perspective can help you to overcome adversity, find joy in life's challenges, and achieve your goals. In this chapter, we will explore the many benefits of an optimistic outlook and how you can cultivate this powerful mindset in your own life.

First and foremost, optimism is linked to better mental health. When you approach life with a positive outlook, you are less likely to experience symptoms of anxiety and depression. You are also more likely to experience higher levels of happiness and well-being. This is because optimism helps you to focus on the positive aspects of your life, rather than dwelling on the negative.

Optimism is also linked to improved physical health. Research has shown that people who are optimistic are less likely to develop chronic health conditions, such as heart disease and diabetes. Additionally, they have a lower risk of dying from heart disease and other serious health problems. This is likely due to the fact that optimism can help to reduce stress levels and promote healthier lifestyle choices, such as exercise and healthy eating.

An optimistic outlook can also have a positive impact on your relationships. When you are optimistic, you are more likable and are often sought after as friends and allies. You are also more likely to build strong relationships with others, which can provide you with a support system during difficult times. Additionally, optimism can help you to communicate more effectively and resolve conflicts in a positive manner.

Another benefit of an optimistic outlook is that it can help you to achieve your goals. When you approach life with a positive perspective, you are more likely to take action towards your goals, persevere in the face of adversity, and bounce back from setbacks. This is because you have a sense of hope and believe that things will work out in the end. Additionally, optimism can help you to maintain a positive outlook even when faced with challenges, which can help you to stay motivated and focused on your goals.

Finally, an optimistic outlook can help you to find joy in life's challenges. When you approach life with a positive perspective, you are more likely to see challenges as opportunities for growth and learning, rather than as insurmountable obstacles. This can help you to find meaning and purpose in life, even in the face of adversity.

In conclusion, the benefits of an optimistic outlook are numerous and far-reaching. By cultivating a positive perspective, you can improve your mental and physical health, strengthen your relationships, achieve your goals, and find joy in life's challenges. Whether you are facing a difficult situation or simply looking to live a happier, healthier life, optimism can be a powerful tool for transformation.

04: Overcoming Negative Thinking and Cultivating a Positive Mindset

Negative thinking patterns can be a major barrier to cultivating an optimistic outlook on life. Whether you struggle with feelings of worry, self-doubt, or cynicism, it can be challenging to find joy and feel confident in the face of adversity. However, with the right strategies and techniques, it is possible to overcome negative thinking and cultivate a positive mindset.

The first step in overcoming negative thinking is to become aware of your thought patterns. Pay attention to the thoughts that go through your mind throughout the day, and notice when you engage in negative self-talk. For example, do you frequently tell yourself that you are not good enough, that you will never succeed, or that you are unlucky? These types of negative thoughts can be incredibly harmful to your mental and emotional well-being.

Once you have become aware of your negative thought patterns, it is important to challenge them. Ask yourself if these thoughts are truly accurate, or if they are based on fear, insecurity, or past experiences. Reframe your negative thoughts in a positive light, and focus on the strengths, qualities, and successes that you possess.

Another effective technique for overcoming negative thinking is to practice gratitude. When you focus on the things that you are grateful for, you are less likely to become trapped in negative thought patterns. Try to make a habit of listing three things that you are grateful for each day, and focus on the positive aspects of your life.

Cultivating a positive mindset also involves developing a growth mindset. This means accepting that challenges and setbacks are an inevitable part of life, but that you can grow and learn from these experiences. When you approach life with a growth mindset, you are less likely to become discouraged when faced with obstacles, and you are more likely to see challenges as opportunities for growth and improvement.

Finally, it is important to surround yourself with positive influences. Spend time with people who are supportive and encouraging, and who help you to see the best in yourself and the world around you. Surrounding yourself with posit-

04: OVERCOMING NEGATIVE THINKING AND CULTIVATING A POSITIVE MINDSET

ive influences can help to counteract the effects of negative thinking, and can help you to maintain a positive outlook even when faced with adversity.

In conclusion, overcoming negative thinking and cultivating a positive mindset is an essential step in developing an optimistic outlook on life. By becoming aware of your negative thought patterns, challenging them, practicing gratitude, developing a growth mindset, and surrounding yourself with positive influences, you can build a foundation of unshakable confidence and find joy in the face of adversity.

05: Reframing Your Thoughts: The Art of Positive Thinking

Positive thinking is a powerful tool that can help you to cultivate an optimistic outlook on life and overcome adversity. However, many people struggle to adopt a positive mindset, as they are stuck in negative thought patterns that are difficult to break. This is where the art of reframing your thoughts comes in.

Reframing is the process of changing the way you think about a situation or experience, so that it becomes more positive and empowering. This can involve looking for the positive aspects of a situation, or finding alternative ways to interpret events. For example, instead of viewing a setback as a failure, you can reframe it as an opportunity to learn and grow.

One of the keys to reframing your thoughts is to challenge your limiting beliefs. These are the thoughts and beliefs that hold you back, and prevent you from seeing the world in a positive light. For example, you might believe that you are not good enough, or that success is not possible for you. By challenging these limiting beliefs, you can begin to adopt a more positive and empowering mindset.

05: REFRAMING YOUR THOUGHTS: THE ART OF POS-ITIVE THINKING

Another key to reframing your thoughts is to focus on solutions, rather than problems. When faced with a challenge, it is easy to get bogged down in the negative aspects of the situation. However, by focusing on solutions, you can tap into your creativity and resourcefulness, and find ways to overcome the obstacles that are in your way.

It is also important to practice gratitude. This involves focusing on the things that you are grateful for, and recognizing the positive aspects of your life. When you focus on gratitude, you are less likely to get caught up in negative thoughts, and you are more likely to feel optimistic and confident.

Finally, it is important to surround yourself with positive influences. This can include friends, family, and other people who support and encourage you. When you are surrounded by positive influences, you are more likely to adopt a positive mindset, and you are less likely to be impacted by negative thoughts and emotions.

In conclusion, reframing your thoughts and adopting a positive mindset is an essential step in developing an optimistic outlook on life. By challenging your limiting beliefs, focusing on solutions, practicing gratitude, and surrounding yourself with positive influences, you can transform your life and find joy, even in the face of adversity.

06: Building Resilience and Coping with Adversity

Adversity is a natural part of life, and it is something that everyone experiences at some point. However, not everyone copes with adversity in the same way. Some people are more resilient, and are able to bounce back from setbacks and challenges, while others struggle to overcome adversity and may become discouraged or defeated.

Building resilience is an important part of cultivating an optimistic outlook on life. Resilience refers to the ability to cope with and recover from adversity, and to bounce back from setbacks and challenges. People who are resilient are better equipped to deal with stress and adversity, and are less likely to be affected by negative thoughts and emotions.

There are several key strategies that can help you to build resilience and cope with adversity. One of the most important is to develop a strong sense of purpose. This involves having a clear understanding of what is important to you, and what you want to achieve in life. When you have a sense of purpose, you are more likely to be motivated and focused, and you are less likely to be impacted by adversity.

Another key strategy is to develop a positive self-image. This involves having a positive and empowering view of yourself, and recognizing your strengths and abilities. When you have a positive self-image, you are more likely to feel confident and self-assured, and you are less likely to be affected by negative thoughts and emotions.

It is also important to cultivate a support network. This involves having friends, family, and other people who you can turn to for support, encouragement, and advice. When you have a strong support network, you are more likely to feel connected and valued, and you are less likely to be affected by adversity.

Another important strategy is to practice self-care. This involves taking care of your physical, emotional, and mental health, and engaging in activities that nourish and support you. When you practice self-care, you are better equipped to cope with stress and adversity, and you are less likely to be affected by negative thoughts and emotions.

Finally, it is important to adopt a growth mindset. This involves viewing challenges and setbacks as opportunities for growth and learning, rather than as failures. When you adopt a growth mindset, you are more likely to be motivated and focused, and you are less likely to be impacted by negative thoughts and emotions.

In conclusion, building resilience and coping with adversity is an essential part of cultivating an optimistic outlook on life. By developing a strong sense of purpose, a positive self-image, a support network, practicing self-care, and adopting a growth mindset, you can overcome adversity and find joy, even in the face of challenges.

07: Finding Joy in the Present Moment

Life can be busy and hectic, and it can be easy to get caught up in worries about the future or regrets about the past. However, when you focus on the present moment, you can experience a sense of peace and contentment that can help you to cultivate a more optimistic outlook on life.

One of the key ways to find joy in the present moment is to practice mindfulness. Mindfulness is the practice of being present and fully engaged in the moment, without judgment or distraction. When you are mindful, you are better able to connect with your thoughts, feelings, and sensations, and you are less likely to be affected by negative thoughts and emotions.

There are several mindfulness practices that you can try to help you find joy in the present moment. One of the simplest is to simply pay attention to your breathing. When you focus on your breath, you can calm your mind and become more aware of your thoughts and feelings.

Another mindfulness practice is to focus on your senses. You can do this by paying attention to what you see, hear, smell, taste, and feel. When you focus on your senses, you can become more connected to the world around you and experience a greater sense of joy and contentment.

Another way to find joy in the present moment is to engage in activities that you enjoy. This might be something as simple as taking a walk in nature, listening to music, or reading a book. When you engage in activities that you enjoy, you are more likely to feel happy and fulfilled, and you are less likely to be affected by negative thoughts and emotions.

It is also important to take time for yourself, and to engage in self-care. This might involve doing something as simple as taking a relaxing bath or meditating, or something more elaborate like a weekend getaway. When you take time for yourself, you are better able to recharge and refresh, and you are less likely to be affected by stress and negativity.

Finally, it is important to cultivate gratitude. Gratitude is the practice of focusing on what you are thankful for in your life. When you cultivate gratitude, you are more likely to experience a sense of joy and contentment, even in the face of adversity.

07: FINDING JOY IN THE PRESENT MOMENT

In conclusion, finding joy in the present moment is an important part of cultivating an optimistic outlook on life. By practicing mindfulness, focusing on your senses, engaging in activities that you enjoy, taking time for yourself, and cultivating gratitude, you can experience a greater sense of happiness and fulfillment, and you can transform your life with unshakable confidence.

08: The Connection Between Gratitude and Optimism

Gratitude and optimism are two important aspects of a positive and fulfilling life. When you cultivate gratitude and optimism, you are more likely to experience joy, happiness, and success, even in the face of adversity.

Gratitude is the practice of focusing on what you are thankful for in your life. When you cultivate gratitude, you are more likely to experience a sense of appreciation and contentment, and you are less likely to be affected by negative thoughts and emotions. Gratitude also helps you to recognize and appreciate the good things in your life, which can help to increase your overall sense of well-being.

Optimism, on the other hand, is the belief that good things will happen in the future. When you are optimistic, you are more likely to approach life's challenges with a positive attitude, and you are less likely to be affected by stress and negativity. Optimism also helps you to believe in yourself and your abilities, which can increase your confidence and help you to achieve your goals.

There is a strong connection between gratitude and optimism. When you cultivate gratitude, you are more likely to experience a sense of happiness and contentment, and this can help to increase your overall sense of optimism. Similarly, when you are optimistic, you are more likely to focus on the good things in your life, and this can help to increase your sense of gratitude.

In order to cultivate gratitude and optimism, it is important to practice gratitude regularly. One simple way to do this is to keep a gratitude journal, in which you write down a few things that you are thankful for each day. You can also make a habit of expressing gratitude to others, either verbally or through acts of kindness.

Another way to cultivate gratitude and optimism is to engage in activities that bring you joy and fulfillment. This might include hobbies, volunteer work, or spending time with friends and family. When you engage in activities that bring you joy, you are more likely to experience a sense of happiness and fulfillment, which can help to increase your overall sense of gratitude and optimism.

Finally, it is important to adopt a positive outlook on life. This might involve focusing on the good things in your life,

08: THE CONNECTION BETWEEN GRATITUDE AND OPTIMISM

approaching challenges with a positive attitude, and believing in yourself and your abilities. When you adopt a positive outlook on life, you are more likely to experience a sense of happiness and success, and you are less likely to be affected by stress and negativity.

In conclusion, the connection between gratitude and optimism is strong and powerful. By cultivating gratitude and optimism, you can transform your life with unshakable confidence, and you can experience greater joy, happiness, and success.

09: The Power of Visualization and Affirmations

Visualization and affirmations are two powerful tools that can help you cultivate an optimistic outlook and transform your life. These techniques involve using your imagination and positive self-talk to create a mental image of the future you desire and reinforce positive beliefs about yourself and the world.

Visualization is the process of creating a mental image of a desired outcome. It allows you to see yourself achieving your goals and experiencing positive emotions, as if they are already happening. By visualizing success, you activate the same brain regions that are activated when you actually experience success. This helps to train your brain to believe that success is possible and sets the foundation for positive change.

For example, if you want to become a successful writer, you might visualize yourself sitting at your desk, typing away on your computer and feeling proud of the work you are producing. You might see yourself receiving positive feedback from your editor and readers, and feeling confident and fulfilled. By visualizing this outcome, you are programming your mind to believe that it is possible, and this belief will motivate you to take action and work towards your goal.

Affirmations are short, positive statements that you repeat to yourself, often in the present tense, as if they are already true. They help to replace negative thoughts and beliefs with positive ones, and reinforce a sense of self-worth and confidence.

For example, if you struggle with low self-esteem, you might repeat affirmations like, "I am worthy of love and respect," "I am capable of achieving my goals," and "I am deserving of happiness and success." By repeating these affirmations daily, you are retraining your brain to believe in yourself and your abilities, which will lead to greater confidence and a more optimistic outlook.

Both visualization and affirmations have been proven to have a powerful impact on mental and emotional well-being. They can help you overcome limiting beliefs, build resilience, and cultivate a positive mindset. By incorporating these techniques into your daily routine, you can harness the power of optimism and transform your life.

10: Setting and Achieving Your Goals with an Optimistic Attitude

One of the key benefits of having an optimistic outlook is that it can help you set and achieve your goals with greater ease. When you are optimistic, you have a sense of hope and confidence in your ability to succeed, which can give you the motivation and drive you need to make your dreams a reality.

However, simply being optimistic is not enough. To make the most of your optimistic outlook, you need to have a clear understanding of what you want to achieve, and develop a plan to get there. This is where goal-setting comes in.

Goal-setting is a powerful tool that allows you to focus your energy and resources on the things that are most important to you. It helps you to clarify your priorities and provides a roadmap for success. When you set goals, you are taking control of your life and creating a path to a better future.

There are several steps you can take to set and achieve your goals with an optimistic attitude:

– Identify your goals: Take some time to reflect on what you want to achieve in life. What do you value most? What makes you happy and fulfilled? Write down your goals, and make sure they are specific, measurable, and achievable.

– Create a plan: Break your goals down into smaller, more manageable steps. Create a timeline for when you want to achieve each step, and identify the resources you will need to succeed.

– Stay focused: Stay focused on your goals, even when you encounter setbacks or challenges. Use visualization and affirmations to reinforce your commitment, and surround yourself with positive, supportive people.

– Celebrate your successes: Acknowledge and celebrate your progress, no matter how small. This will help you maintain your momentum and stay motivated.

– Adjust your approach: If you encounter obstacles or obstacles that prevent you from achieving your goals, don't be discouraged. Instead, adjust your approach and find new ways to overcome the challenges.

By following these steps, you can set and achieve your goals with an optimistic attitude, and experience the benefits of a positive outlook on life. With hard work, determination, and a healthy dose of optimism, you can create a future that is filled with joy, success, and fulfillment.

11: The Impact of Optimism on Relationships

Optimism is not just a state of mind that can bring benefits to your own life, but also to the people around you, especially those you have close relationships with. An optimistic outlook has the power to change the way you interact with others and the way they interact with you, leading to more positive and fulfilling relationships. In this chapter, we will explore the impact of optimism on relationships and how it can bring more joy, love, and connection into your life.

First of all, optimism helps you maintain a positive outlook in your relationships. When you are optimistic, you are less likely to see things in a negative light, and more likely to find the good in any situation. This positive outlook can have a profound impact on your relationships. When you approach your relationships with a positive attitude, you are less likely to argue or get upset when things don't go your way. Instead, you will be more open to finding solutions and working together to find a way forward.

Moreover, optimism can also help improve communication in your relationships. When you are optimistic, you are more likely to approach conversations with a positive attitude, and you are more likely to listen actively to what the other person is saying. This leads to better understanding and more meaningful connections. When you approach conversations with a positive attitude, you also create a safe and supportive environment for open and honest communication, leading to better understanding and more meaningful connections.

Another way that optimism can impact your relationships is by creating a more positive environment. Optimistic people tend to bring more positivity and joy into their relationships. When you approach your relationships with an optimistic outlook, you are more likely to find joy in spending time with the people you care about, and you are also more likely to bring a sense of positivity and happiness into your relationships.

In conclusion, optimism has a significant impact on relationships, and it can help you build stronger, more meaningful connections with the people you care about. When you approach your relationships with an optimistic outlook, you are more likely to communicate effectively, create a positive environment, and find joy in the time you spend with the people you love. Remember, relationships are one

11: THE IMPACT OF OPTIMISM ON RELATIONSHIPS

of the most important things in life, and optimism can help you create and maintain the best relationships possible.

12: The Benefits of Positive Social Connections

Introduction:

Positive social connections are crucial to our well-being and can play a significant role in cultivating an optimistic outlook on life. Our relationships with others, whether it be family, friends, or coworkers, can either provide support and encouragement or bring negativity and stress into our lives. In this chapter, we'll explore the benefits of positive social connections and how they contribute to our overall happiness and success.

The Importance of Positive Social Connections:

Studies have shown that strong social connections play a crucial role in reducing stress and improving mental health. When we feel connected to others, we feel more secure and confident, which can lead to increased self-esteem and a more positive outlook on life. Positive social connections can also help us to cope with adversity and challenges, as we have a support system to turn to during difficult times.

Boosting Our Physical Health:

12: THE BENEFITS OF POSITIVE SOCIAL CONNEC-TIONS

Positive social connections can also have a significant impact on our physical health. Research has shown that people with strong social connections have a lower risk of developing chronic illnesses, such as heart disease, and are more likely to recover quickly from illness or injury. This is due to the fact that positive relationships can help to reduce stress levels, which can have negative effects on our physical health.

Enhancing Our Mental Health:

Positive social connections can also help to improve our mental health by providing us with a sense of belonging and purpose. When we feel connected to others, we feel more confident and secure, which can help to reduce feelings of anxiety and depression. In addition, positive social connections can provide us with a sense of identity, which can help to improve our overall self-esteem and confidence.

Building Strong Relationships:

Building strong relationships takes time, effort, and commitment. Some key factors to consider when building positive social connections include being an active listener, being empathetic, and being open and honest with others. It's also important to seek out opportunities to connect with others, such as through volunteer work, clubs, or social events.

Conclusion:

In conclusion, positive social connections are a crucial part of our lives and can have a significant impact on our overall happiness and well-being. By focusing on building strong relationships, we can cultivate an optimistic outlook on life and find joy and fulfillment in our interactions with others. Whether it's through family, friends, or social events, the benefits of positive social connections are numerous, and they are an essential aspect of living a happy and fulfilling life.

13: The Role of Forgiveness in Cultivating Optimism

Introduction:

Forgiveness is a powerful tool in cultivating optimism and transforming your life. It has the ability to release negative emotions, such as anger, resentment, and bitterness, and replace them with feelings of peace and joy. In this chapter, we will explore the role of forgiveness in developing an optimistic outlook and how it can positively impact your life.

The Power of Forgiveness:

Forgiveness is not about forgetting the past or condoning harmful actions. Instead, it is about releasing the hold that negative emotions have on you and moving forward with a positive outlook. By forgiving others, you free yourself from the chains of anger and resentment, allowing you to live in the present moment and embrace a brighter future. This can lead to improved physical and mental health, as well as stronger and more fulfilling relationships.

The Benefits of Forgiveness:

Forgiveness has been shown to have a number of benefits

for both the person who forgives and the person being for-given. For the person who forgives, it can reduce stress, anxiety, and depression, while also improving overall well-being. On the other hand, for the person being forgiven, it can bring closure and a sense of peace, which can help to heal past wounds and move forward in a positive direction.

Overcoming Resistance to Forgiveness:

Forgiving others can be difficult, especially when the harm that was done was severe or ongoing. However, it is import-ant to remember that forgiveness is not about forgetting or excusing harmful actions, but rather about releasing negat-ive emotions and embracing a positive outlook. To help overcome resistance to forgiveness, it can be helpful to practice self-reflection and understand the reasons behind your emotions. You may also consider seeking support from friends, family, or a therapist.

The Process of Forgiveness:

Forgiveness is a process that may take time, but with prac-tice and patience, it is possible to cultivate a forgiving heart. It may involve acknowledging the hurt that was caused, expressing your feelings, and releasing negative emotions. It may also involve letting go of any grudges or resentment and replacing them with compassion and understanding.

Conclusion:

Forgiveness is a key component of cultivating an optimistic outlook and transforming your life. By releasing negative emotions and embracing a positive attitude, you can improve your physical and mental health, strengthen your relationships, and achieve greater success. Remember that forgiveness is a process, and with time and patience, you can learn to forgive and embrace a brighter future.

14: Overcoming Fear and Embracing Change

Fear and change are two of the most common challenges that people face in life. Fear can be debilitating and hold us back from achieving our goals and living the life we want. Change, on the other hand, is a natural part of life, but it can also be unsettling and bring uncertainty. However, with an optimistic attitude, we can overcome fear and embrace change. In this chapter, we will explore the relationship between fear and change and how optimism can help us to overcome both.

Fear is a natural human emotion that is triggered by a perceived threat. It can take many forms, such as fear of failure, fear of the unknown, or fear of loss. While fear can be a helpful tool for keeping us safe, it can also be limiting when it holds us back from pursuing our goals and dreams.

Change, on the other hand, can also be a source of fear. Change can bring uncertainty and discomfort, which can trigger feelings of fear. Whether it's a change in our personal life, such as a new job or a move to a new city, or a change in the world around us, such as a pandemic or a natural disaster, change can be unsettling.

However, with an optimistic attitude, we can learn to embrace change and overcome fear. When we view change as an opportunity for growth and personal development, it becomes less daunting. When we focus on the possibilities instead of the risks, we can overcome the fear that change often brings.

Similarly, when we adopt an optimistic outlook, we can overcome the fear of failure. Rather than dwelling on the potential for failure, we can focus on the opportunities for success. When we view failure as a learning opportunity, rather than a defeat, we can build resilience and develop the confidence to take risks and pursue our goals.

In addition to overcoming fear, optimism can also help us to embrace change. When we view change as a positive opportunity, we are more likely to see the potential benefits and opportunities that come with it. With an optimistic outlook, we can approach change with confidence, knowing that we have the strength and resilience to navigate any challenges that may arise.

In conclusion, fear and change are natural parts of life that can be overwhelming and limiting. However, with an optimistic attitude, we can overcome fear and embrace change. By focusing on the possibilities and opportunities, we can develop the resilience and confidence needed to achieve our goals and live a fulfilling life.

15: The Importance of Self-Care in Maintaining Optimism

Self-care is an essential aspect of maintaining an optimistic outlook and overall well-being. In this chapter, we will explore the role of self-care in fostering a positive and confident attitude.

Self-care encompasses a wide range of activities that promote physical, mental, and emotional health. This can include things like exercise, healthy eating, meditation, and spending time with loved ones. By taking care of ourselves, we can recharge and feel better equipped to handle the challenges that come our way.

In addition to its physical benefits, self-care can also have a profound impact on our mental and emotional health. It can help us manage stress, reduce anxiety, and promote feelings of happiness and well-being. When we feel good about ourselves, it becomes easier to have an optimistic outlook and approach life with confidence.

One of the most important aspects of self-care is making time for it in our busy schedules. It's easy to put our own needs aside when we're focused on work, family, and other responsibilities. However, it's important to remember that taking care of ourselves is not a luxury, but a necessity. When we invest in ourselves, we become better equipped to handle the challenges that come our way and maintain an optimistic outlook.

There are many different ways to incorporate self-care into your life. It can be as simple as taking a relaxing bath, going for a walk in nature, or taking a yoga class. Whatever form it takes, it's important to make self-care a priority and to find activities that you enjoy and that help you feel refreshed and recharged.

In conclusion, self-care is an important aspect of maintaining an optimistic outlook and overall well-being. By taking care of our physical, mental, and emotional health, we can recharge, reduce stress, and feel better equipped to handle the challenges that come our way. So make time for self-care, invest in yourself, and watch as your confidence and optimism grow.

16: Mindfulness and the Pursuit of Happiness

The pursuit of happiness is a universal human goal that has been the subject of countless philosophical, religious and scientific debates throughout history. In recent years, mindfulness has become an increasingly popular way to cultivate happiness, reduce stress and increase wellbeing. In this chapter, we will explore the connection between mindfulness and optimism, and how practicing mindfulness can help you cultivate a more positive outlook on life.

Mindfulness is a mental state achieved by focusing one's awareness on the present moment, while calmly acknowledging and accepting one's feelings, thoughts, and bodily sensations. It is an ancient practice that has been around for thousands of years, but has recently gained popularity as a tool for improving mental health and overall wellbeing. The benefits of mindfulness are numerous and well-documented, including reduced stress, increased emotional regulation, and improved cognitive function.

In terms of its impact on optimism, mindfulness helps us to become more aware of our thoughts and feelings, and to see them in a more objective light. When we are mindful, we are

45

less likely to be swept away by negative thoughts and emotions, and more likely to respond to difficult situations with a sense of equanimity and calm. This, in turn, can lead to greater optimism and resilience in the face of adversity.

One of the key benefits of mindfulness is that it helps us to develop a more positive outlook on life. When we are mindful, we are able to focus on the present moment, instead of dwelling on the past or worrying about the future. This helps us to appreciate the small things in life and to find joy in everyday experiences. Additionally, mindfulness can help us to cultivate a more grateful and appreciative attitude towards life. By focusing on the present moment and appreciating what we have, we can develop a greater sense of contentment and satisfaction, which can lead to increased happiness and well-being.

Another important aspect of mindfulness is its ability to increase our self-awareness. When we are mindful, we become more aware of our thoughts, feelings, and actions, which can help us to better understand ourselves and to make positive changes in our lives. This increased self-awareness can also lead to greater self-compassion, which is crucial for maintaining a positive outlook on life. By being kind and compassionate towards ourselves, we can reduce negative self-talk and cultivate a more optimistic attitude.

In conclusion, mindfulness is a powerful tool for cultivating optimism and increasing happiness and well-being. By focusing on the present moment and becoming more aware of our thoughts, feelings and actions, we can develop a more positive outlook on life, increase our resilience in the face of adversity, and find joy in the everyday. By incorporating mindfulness into your daily life, you can transform your life with unshakable confidence and the power of optimism.

17: The Benefits of Meditation and Relaxation Techniques

The importance of relaxation and stress reduction in our daily lives cannot be overstated. This is why meditation and other relaxation techniques have been practiced for thousands of years and have become a staple in many cultures around the world. These techniques offer a wide range of benefits that can help you cultivate a more optimistic outlook and maintain a positive mindset.

One of the primary benefits of meditation is that it helps to calm the mind and reduce stress. Stress is a major contributor to negativity, anxiety, and depression, and can have a profound impact on our health and wellbeing. Through meditation, you can learn to quiet the mind and control your thoughts, which can help you to reduce stress and feel more relaxed. This, in turn, can improve your mood, boost your energy levels, and increase your sense of overall wellbeing.

Another benefit of meditation is that it can help you to cultivate a greater sense of self-awareness. When you meditate, you focus your attention inward, which can help you to become more aware of your thoughts, feelings, and emotions.

17: THE BENEFITS OF MEDITATION AND RELAXATION TECHNIQUES

This can be especially useful when dealing with negative thoughts or feelings, as it can help you to recognize when these thoughts are taking hold and take steps to reframe them.

Meditation can also help you to develop more compassion and empathy towards yourself and others. When you take time to focus inward, you can better understand your own thoughts, feelings, and motivations, and this understanding can translate into greater compassion for others. Additionally, studies have shown that meditation can increase levels of compassion, kindness, and empathy in people, which can help to improve relationships and foster a more optimistic outlook.

Relaxation techniques like yoga and deep breathing can also be incredibly beneficial in promoting optimism. These techniques help to release tension in the body, calm the mind, and promote feelings of peace and calm. Additionally, yoga has been shown to boost mood and increase feelings of happiness, as well as improve sleep quality, which can also contribute to a more optimistic outlook.

It is important to note that while meditation and relaxation

17: THE BENEFITS OF MEDITATION AND RELAXATION TECHNIQUES

techniques can be incredibly beneficial, they are not a quick fix or a cure-all solution. However, when practiced regularly, they can become an integral part of your self-care routine and help you to cultivate a more optimistic outlook and maintain a positive mindset.

In conclusion, meditation and relaxation techniques can offer a range of benefits that can help you cultivate a more optimistic outlook and maintain a positive mindset. Whether you prefer to practice meditation, yoga, deep breathing, or other relaxation techniques, incorporating these practices into your daily routine can help you to reduce stress, improve your mood, and increase your sense of overall well-being. So why not take the time to explore these techniques today and discover the many benefits that they can offer you on your journey towards a more optimistic and confident life.

18: The Power of Movement: The Physical Benefits of Optimism

Introduction:

The connection between physical movement and optimism is often overlooked, but it is a critical component of overall well-being. The benefits of physical activity are well-known, but did you know that incorporating physical movement into your daily routine can also enhance your optimism? Studies have shown that regular physical activity can boost mood, reduce stress, and even improve self-esteem, all of which contribute to a more optimistic outlook on life.

The Benefits of Movement:

– Boosts Mood: Exercise is known to release endorphins, which are the body's natural mood enhancers. When you engage in physical activity, these endorphins are released into your bloodstream, giving you a natural high and improving your mood. Regular exercise can also help regulate your sleep patterns, which can also contribute to a better mood.

– Reduces Stress: Exercise is an excellent stress-reliever.

18: THE POWER OF MOVEMENT: THE PHYSICAL BENE-FITS OF OPTIMISM

When you're feeling overwhelmed or stressed, engaging in physical activity can help clear your mind and reduce the levels of stress hormones in your body. This reduction in stress can lead to a more optimistic outlook on life.

– Improves Self-Esteem: Regular physical activity can also boost self-esteem. When you see yourself making progress in your fitness journey, you'll feel a sense of pride and accomplishment, which can increase your self-esteem and improve your overall confidence.

– Increases Energy: Regular physical activity can also increase energy levels. When you're feeling sluggish or tired, engaging in physical activity can give you a burst of energy and help you feel more awake and alert. This increased energy can help you tackle the day with a more positive attitude.

– Promotes Relaxation: Exercise can also promote relaxation. When you're feeling anxious or stressed, physical activity can help you calm down and relax. This relaxed state can lead to a more optimistic outlook on life.

How to Incorporate Movement into Your Routine:

18: THE POWER OF MOVEMENT: THE PHYSICAL BENE-FITS OF OPTIMISM

The key to reaping the benefits of physical movement is to make it a regular part of your routine. Here are some tips to help you get started:

– Find an activity you enjoy: It's important to find an activity that you enjoy. Whether it's running, yoga, or swimming, find an activity that you look forward to doing each day.

– Make a schedule: Once you've found an activity you enjoy, make a schedule and stick to it. Whether it's 30 minutes each day or an hour three times a week, make a commitment to engage in physical activity regularly.

– Get a workout partner: Having a workout partner can help keep you accountable and motivated. Find someone who shares your passion for physical activity and commit to working out together regularly.

– Experiment: Don't be afraid to experiment with different activities to find what works best for you. Try different forms of exercise, such as dance classes or outdoor activities, until you find what you enjoy the most.

Conclusion:

18: THE POWER OF MOVEMENT: THE PHYSICAL BENE-FITS OF OPTIMISM

The benefits of physical activity on optimism are numerous and often overlooked. Regular physical movement can boost mood, reduce stress, improve self-esteem, increase energy, and promote relaxation, all of which contribute to a more optimistic outlook on life. So, if you're looking to transform your life with unshakable confidence, make physical movement a regular part of your routine and watch as your optimism grows stronger each day.

19: The Connection Between Optimism and a Healthy Lifestyle

Introduction:

We all know that being optimistic can have a positive impact on our mental and emotional well-being, but did you know that it can also have a significant impact on our physical health? The connection between optimism and a healthy lifestyle is undeniable, and this chapter will explore the many ways in which optimism can lead to a healthier and happier life.

The Physical Benefits of Optimism:

Studies have shown that individuals who exhibit optimistic tendencies have a reduced risk of numerous physical health problems, including heart disease, stroke, and certain types of cancer. This is because optimism is often associated with healthier behaviors, such as regular exercise, a healthy diet, and avoiding unhealthy habits like smoking and excessive alcohol consumption.

In addition to reducing the risk of certain health problems, optimism has also been shown to improve physical recovery from illness or injury. Optimistic individuals tend to have a more positive outlook on life and are more likely to seek medical treatment when necessary, which can lead to faster and more complete recoveries. Furthermore, optimism has been linked to improved immune function, which can help the body fight off illness and disease more effectively.

The Connection Between Optimism and Exercise:

One of the key ways in which optimism can lead to a healthier lifestyle is through its connection to exercise. Optimistic individuals are more likely to engage in regular physical activity, which has numerous health benefits, including improved cardiovascular function, stronger bones, and a healthier body weight. Additionally, exercise has been shown to reduce stress and improve mood, which can further enhance the benefits of optimism.

The Connection Between Optimism and Diet:

Another important aspect of a healthy lifestyle is a balanced and nutritious diet, and optimism can play a role in this as well. Optimistic individuals are more likely to make healthy food choices and are less likely to engage in unhealthy eating habits, such as overeating or skipping meals. By making healthier food choices, optimistic individuals can reduce their risk of numerous health problems, including obesity, heart disease, and type 2 diabetes.

The Connection Between Optimism and Stress Management:

In addition to the physical benefits of optimism, it can also play a role in managing stress and promoting overall well-being. Optimistic individuals are often better equipped to handle stress and are less likely to experience anxiety and depression. This is because they tend to focus on the positive aspects of life and are more resilient in the face of adversity. Furthermore, they are more likely to engage in healthy stress-management techniques, such as exercise, meditation, and relaxation, which can further enhance the benefits of optimism.

Conclusion:

In conclusion, the connection between optimism and a healthy lifestyle is undeniable. By embracing an optimistic outlook on life, individuals can reduce their risk of numerous health problems, improve physical recovery from illness or injury, and achieve a greater level of well-being. Whether through exercise, diet, stress management, or other means, optimism can help individuals lead happier and healthier lives. So, let us embrace the power of optimism and make positive changes in our lives today.

20: The Benefits of Nature and Outdoor Activities for Your Mental Health

One of the key components to cultivating and maintaining a positive, optimistic outlook on life is to engage in activities that promote physical and mental well-being. And one of the simplest and most effective ways to do this is to spend time in nature. Engaging in outdoor activities and immersing yourself in the natural world has been shown to have numerous benefits for our mental health and well-being, including reducing stress, improving mood, and increasing feelings of happiness and optimism.

Studies have shown that exposure to nature can help to reduce levels of cortisol, the stress hormone, in our bodies. This reduction in cortisol has been linked to lower levels of anxiety and depression, as well as increased feelings of well-being and happiness. Spending time in nature has also been shown to improve focus and attention, allowing you to better manage daily stress and distractions. This increased focus can also help you to be more productive and effective in your daily tasks and goals.

20: THE BENEFITS OF NATURE AND OUTDOOR ACTIV-
ITIES FOR YOUR MENTAL HEALTH

In addition to the physical benefits of spending time in nature, there are also numerous emotional and psychological benefits. Immersing yourself in nature has been shown to increase feelings of connectedness and interdependence, which can lead to greater feelings of joy and satisfaction. Spending time in nature can also help to increase your sense of gratitude and appreciation for the world around you, which can lead to greater feelings of happiness and contentment.

One of the best ways to experience the benefits of nature is through outdoor activities such as hiking, camping, or even simply going for a walk in the park. Engaging in physical activity in nature has been shown to have even greater benefits for our mental and emotional well-being than simply being in nature. The combination of physical activity, fresh air, and natural beauty has been shown to have a powerful impact on our mood and outlook, leading to greater feelings of optimism and joy.

Incorporating outdoor activities and nature into your daily routine can be as simple as taking a daily walk in a nearby park or spending time in your backyard garden. Find activities that you enjoy and make them a regular part of your routine. Whether it's hiking, camping, or simply spending time in a nearby park, make time for nature and see the positive impact it can have on your mental and emotional well-being.

In conclusion, spending time in nature and engaging in outdoor activities is a simple and effective way to cultivate a positive, optimistic outlook on life. The physical and mental benefits of nature and outdoor activities are numerous, and can help you to reduce stress, improve your mood, and increase feelings of happiness and well-being. So, get outside, get active, and experience the power of nature for yourself. You will be amazed at the positive impact it can have on your life.

21: The Importance of Sleep for Maintaining Optimism

Sleep is a critical component of our overall health and well-being, and it is essential for maintaining an optimistic outlook on life. Research has shown that individuals who get adequate sleep are more likely to have a positive outlook, better moods, and higher levels of energy and productivity. In contrast, lack of sleep has been linked to negative emotions, decreased motivation, and a higher risk of depression and anxiety.

In order to understand the connection between sleep and optimism, it is important to understand the role that sleep plays in our physical and mental health. During sleep, our bodies undergo a number of important processes, including repairing and restoring our cells, strengthening our immune system, and consolidating our memories. Additionally, sleep has been shown to play a crucial role in regulating our mood and emotional well-being.

When we are well-rested, we are more likely to feel energetic and motivated, and our mood is more stable and positive. This is due in part to the fact that sleep helps to regulate the levels of hormones and neurotransmitters in our bodies that are responsible for our emotional state. For example, lack of sleep can lead to a decrease in the production of serotonin, a hormone that helps regulate our mood and feelings of happiness.

Additionally, sleep has been shown to play a crucial role in helping us process and regulate our emotions. During sleep, our brains are able to consolidate and process the experiences and emotions of the day, which can help us to better manage and understand our emotional state. This, in turn, can lead to a more positive outlook and a greater sense of well-being.

One of the ways that sleep helps us to maintain an optimistic outlook is by reducing stress and anxiety. Chronic stress and anxiety can take a toll on our mental and physical health, leading to feelings of hopelessness and depression. However, sleep has been shown to reduce the levels of cortisol, a hormone that is associated with stress, in our bodies. By reducing stress and anxiety, sleep can help to prevent feelings of hopelessness and depression, and promote a more positive outlook.

In conclusion, sleep is a critical component of our overall

21: THE IMPORTANCE OF SLEEP FOR MAINTAINING OPTIMISM

health and well-being, and it plays a crucial role in maintaining an optimistic outlook on life. By providing our bodies with the rest and restoration that it needs, sleep can help us to feel more energetic, motivated, and positive, and can help us to better manage and regulate our emotions. To maintain an optimistic outlook, it is important to make sleep a priority, and to aim for at least 7-8 hours of quality sleep each night. By doing so, you can help to ensure that you are well-rested and able to face each day with an unshakable confidence and an optimistic attitude.

22: The Role of Humor and Laughter in Boosting Optimism

Humor and laughter have been recognized as essential components of a happy and fulfilling life for centuries. From the ancient Greek philosopher Aristotle, who claimed that "the joy of the mind is the measure of its strength," to modern-day research on the health benefits of laughter, there is no denying the power of humor and laughter in boosting optimism.

Laughter has been proven to have numerous physical and psychological benefits, including reducing stress and anxiety, boosting immunity, improving mood, and even increasing longevity. In addition, humor has the ability to bring people together, foster positive social connections, and provide a much-needed distraction from life's challenges.

When it comes to optimism, laughter has a powerful impact. Research has shown that humor and laughter can increase our sense of well-being and promote a positive outlook on life. Laughter can help us shift our focus from negative thoughts and situations to a more positive perspective, and in doing so, promote feelings of happiness and contentment.

22: THE ROLE OF HUMOR AND LAUGHTER IN BOOST-ING OPTIMISM

One of the reasons why humor and laughter are so effective in promoting optimism is that they can help us see things in a different light. A good joke or a funny story can help us gain a fresh perspective on a difficult situation, allowing us to see the absurdity of the situation and release some of the tension and stress we may be feeling. This shift in perspective can lead to a more positive outlook on life and an increase in optimism.

Moreover, humor can help us cultivate resilience in the face of adversity. It can provide us with a sense of perspective and help us keep things in perspective, even in challenging times. Humor has the ability to bring some levity to difficult situations, making it easier for us to handle them with grace and optimism.

In addition to its role in boosting optimism, humor and laughter can also play an important role in building and maintaining strong relationships. Humor is a powerful tool for breaking down barriers and creating bonds between people. It can help us connect with others on a deeper level, foster positive social connections, and promote a sense of community.

22: THE ROLE OF HUMOR AND LAUGHTER IN BOOSTING OPTIMISM

To maximize the benefits of humor and laughter in promoting optimism, it is important to make time for them in our daily lives. This could mean seeking out comedy shows, reading funny books or articles, or simply spending time with friends and family who make us laugh. It is also important to engage in activities that bring us joy and make us feel good, such as hobbies and interests that bring a smile to our faces.

In conclusion, humor and laughter play a significant role in boosting optimism and promoting a positive outlook on life. Whether it's through a good joke or a funny story, laughter has the power to shift our focus, bring some levity to difficult situations, and increase our sense of well-being. By making time for humor and laughter in our daily lives, we can cultivate resilience, foster positive relationships, and live a happier, more fulfilling life.

23: The Benefits of Giving Back and Helping Others

In this chapter, we will delve into the impact that giving back and helping others can have on our overall sense of well-being and optimism. We will explore the various ways in which we can engage in acts of kindness and generosity, and why these activities can have such a profound effect on our mental and emotional health.

One of the key benefits of giving back and helping others is that it can help to reduce stress and anxiety. When we engage in acts of kindness and generosity, our focus shifts away from our own worries and problems, and towards the needs of others. This can help to create a sense of perspective, and can reduce feelings of hopelessness and helplessness that can be associated with stress and anxiety.

Another important benefit of giving back and helping others is that it can boost our sense of self-esteem and confidence. By making a positive impact in the lives of others, we can feel good about ourselves and our place in the world. This can help to counteract feelings of low self-worth, and can help to build a strong foundation of confidence that can be drawn upon in times of need.

23: THE BENEFITS OF GIVING BACK AND HELPING OTHERS

Giving back and helping others can also have a profound impact on our emotional well-being. When we engage in acts of kindness and generosity, we are making a positive difference in the world, and this can have a ripple effect that extends far beyond our own individual impact. By contributing to the well-being of others, we can create a positive chain reaction that can help to spread optimism and happiness throughout our communities and beyond.

There are many different ways in which we can engage in acts of giving back and helping others. Some examples might include volunteering at a local food bank, helping to care for elderly or disabled neighbors, donating money to charitable organizations, or simply reaching out to offer a kind word or gesture to someone who is struggling.

It is important to note that giving back and helping others can also have practical benefits. For example, volunteering can help to develop new skills and build professional networks. By engaging in acts of kindness and generosity, we can also form new relationships and strengthen existing ones, which can help to foster a sense of connection and support.

23: THE BENEFITS OF GIVING BACK AND HELPING OTHERS

In conclusion, the benefits of giving back and helping others are numerous and far-reaching. By making a positive impact in the lives of others, we can reduce stress and anxiety, boost our self-esteem and confidence, improve our emotional well-being, and form new relationships and connections. By embracing the power of optimism, and incorporating acts of kindness and generosity into our daily lives, we can help to create a brighter, more hopeful future for ourselves and for those around us.

24: Overcoming Procrastination with an Optimistic Attitude

Procrastination is a common challenge that can negatively impact all areas of our lives. Whether it's avoiding important tasks at work, postponing important decisions, or neglecting our health and well-being, procrastination can prevent us from reaching our full potential. However, with an optimistic attitude, you can overcome this common challenge and achieve your goals.

An optimistic attitude can help you approach tasks with a positive outlook, rather than dreading the work involved. When you have a positive attitude, you're more likely to take action and make progress, rather than putting things off. An optimistic attitude can also give you the confidence to tackle challenges, knowing that you have the skills and resources to succeed.

One effective technique for overcoming procrastination is to set clear, specific, and achievable goals. When you have a clear understanding of what you want to accomplish, it's easier to stay focused and motivated. Additionally, break down larger goals into smaller, manageable tasks, and reward yourself for each accomplishment along the way. Celebrating small victories can help you stay motivated and maintain your optimistic attitude.

Another important aspect of overcoming procrastination is to establish a routine and stick to it. When you have a set schedule, you're more likely to make time for important tasks and less likely to put things off. Additionally, creating a supportive environment and surrounding yourself with positive, motivated people can help you stay on track and achieve your goals.

It's also important to address any underlying causes of procrastination, such as fear of failure, low self-esteem, or a lack of motivation. By addressing these underlying issues, you can build a stronger foundation for success and overcome procrastination for good.

Finally, don't be too hard on yourself if you fall back into old habits. It takes time and effort to overcome procrastination, and setbacks are a natural part of the process. Instead of beating yourself up, focus on what you can learn from each setback, and use this knowledge to make positive changes moving forward.

24: OVERCOMING PROCRASTINATION WITH AN OPTIMISTIC ATTITUDE

In conclusion, overcoming procrastination with an optimistic attitude is an achievable goal. By setting clear goals, establishing a routine, addressing underlying causes, and being kind to yourself, you can overcome procrastination and achieve the success you deserve. With an optimistic attitude, you can transform your life and unlock your full potential.

25: The Benefits of Mindful Communication

In our fast-paced world, communication has become increasingly important. It's not just what we say, but how we say it that matters. And in many cases, the way we communicate can make all the difference in our relationships, both personal and professional. This is where mindfulness comes in. When we are mindful in our communication, we are more likely to be present in the moment, listen attentively, and respond in a way that is aligned with our values and goals. In this chapter, we will explore the benefits of mindful communication and how it can help us cultivate a more optimistic attitude in our lives.

The first benefit of mindful communication is improved relationships. When we are mindful in our communication, we are more likely to listen deeply and respond in a way that is respectful and compassionate. This can help us build deeper and more meaningful relationships with those around us. For example, if you are having a disagreement with someone, taking a moment to step back and listen to their perspective with an open mind can help you understand their point of view and come to a resolution that is mutually beneficial.

The second benefit of mindful communication is improved decision-making. When we are mindful in our communication, we are less likely to react impulsively and more likely to consider all of our options before making a decision. This can help us make decisions that are aligned with our values and goals, and ultimately lead to more positive outcomes. For example, if you are faced with a difficult decision, taking a moment to reflect on your values and what is important to you can help you make a decision that is in line with your goals.

The third benefit of mindful communication is reduced stress and anxiety. When we are mindful in our communication, we are more likely to communicate in a way that is calm and centered, which can help us reduce our stress and anxiety levels. For example, if you are feeling overwhelmed, taking a moment to focus on your breath and communicate with those around you in a calm and centered manner can help you feel more relaxed and at ease.

The fourth benefit of mindful communication is improved self-awareness. When we are mindful in our communication, we are more likely to be aware of our own thoughts and feelings, and to be able to identify and manage them in a healthy way. For example, if you are feeling frustrated, taking a moment to reflect on your thoughts and feelings can help you identify what is causing your frustration and find a way to manage it in a healthy way.

In conclusion, mindful communication is a powerful tool for cultivating an optimistic attitude in our lives. By improving our relationships, decision-making, reducing stress and anxiety, and improving self-awareness, we can live our lives with greater confidence, joy, and success. To start practicing mindful communication, try taking a moment to pause before you respond in a conversation, and focus on listening deeply to the person speaking to you. As you practice, you will find that your communication becomes more mindful and that your relationships, decision-making, and overall well-being improve as a result.

26: The Power of Positive Self-Talk

Positive self-talk, or talking to oneself in a positive and encouraging manner, is an incredibly powerful tool for maintaining optimism and promoting well-being. When we engage in negative self-talk, we often focus on our flaws and shortcomings, and this can lead to feelings of insecurity, low self-esteem, and even depression. On the other hand, positive self-talk can help us to build confidence, focus on our strengths, and cultivate a more optimistic outlook.

Positive self-talk involves paying attention to the words we use when we speak to ourselves, and making a conscious effort to replace negative or critical self-talk with more encouraging and supportive statements. This can be as simple as repeating affirmations or positive mantras, or taking time each day to reflect on our accomplishments and strengths.

One of the benefits of positive self-talk is that it helps to shift our focus away from negative experiences and towards the positive aspects of our lives. When we are able to focus on the positive, we are more likely to experience feelings of gratitude, contentment, and joy. In addition, positive self-talk can also help us to build resilience, as it helps us to develop a more optimistic and hopeful outlook, even in the face of adversity.

Another benefit of positive self-talk is that it can help us to cultivate a more confident and self-assured demeanor. When we talk to ourselves in a positive and confident manner, we are sending a message to our subconscious that we believe in ourselves and our abilities. This can help us to overcome fears and doubts, and to approach challenges with greater resolve.

Finally, positive self-talk can also have a significant impact on our relationships. When we are more confident and self-assured, we are more likely to interact with others in a positive and effective manner. This can help us to build stronger, more supportive relationships, and to foster a more positive and encouraging social network.

In conclusion, the power of positive self-talk should not be underestimated. By engaging in positive self-talk on a regular basis, we can cultivate a more optimistic and confident outlook, build resilience, and improve our relationships with others. So, if you want to transform your life with unshakable confidence, start by paying attention to the words you use when you talk to yourself, and make a conscious effort to shift your focus towards the positive.

27: The Importance of Mindful Listening

In our fast-paced and often noisy world, it can be difficult to listen to others and truly understand what they're saying. However, the ability to listen mindfully is an important component of cultivating optimism and building positive relationships. Mindful listening involves paying full attention to the person speaking, without judgment or distraction. By doing so, you are able to understand their perspective, validate their feelings, and build trust.

One of the key benefits of mindful listening is that it helps to reduce misunderstandings and conflicts. When you listen actively and without distractions, you are more likely to accurately understand the person's message, reducing the likelihood of miscommunication. This can help to prevent conflicts and resolve any issues that may arise in your relationships.

In addition to reducing misunderstandings and conflicts, mindful listening can also help to build stronger relationships. When someone feels heard and understood, they are more likely to trust you and feel connected to you. This can lead to deeper and more meaningful relationships, which can bring joy and fulfillment to your life.

Another benefit of mindful listening is that it can help to reduce stress and anxiety. When we are fully present in the moment, our minds are not consumed with worries or distractions. This can help us to feel more relaxed and calm, reducing feelings of stress and anxiety.

Mindful listening can also be a powerful tool for personal growth. When you listen deeply to others, you are able to gain new insights and perspectives that can broaden your understanding of the world and help you to grow as a person. This can lead to greater self-awareness and a deeper understanding of yourself and others.

Finally, mindful listening can help to build empathy and compassion. When we listen deeply to others, we are able to understand their experiences and feelings, which can help us to develop empathy and compassion. This can lead to greater kindness and understanding in our relationships, and a more positive and optimistic outlook on life.

In conclusion, the ability to listen mindfully is an important aspect of cultivating optimism and building positive relationships. By actively listening to others, you can reduce misunderstandings and conflicts, build stronger relation-ships, reduce stress and anxiety, foster personal growth, and build empathy and compassion. So, next time you find yourself in a conversation, take a deep breath, clear your mind, and listen deeply to what the other person has to say. Your relationships, and your outlook on life, will thank you for it.

28: The Benefits of Building Strong Relationships with Friends and Family

The human connection is one of the most fundamental aspects of our lives. Whether it's with friends, family, or romantic partners, our relationships can have a profound impact on our well-being, confidence, and overall happiness. In this chapter, we will explore the benefits of building strong relationships with those closest to us and how these connections can help us cultivate and maintain an optimistic outlook on life.

One of the most significant benefits of having strong relationships with friends and family is the sense of belonging and connectedness that they provide. When we feel connected to others, we are less likely to feel isolated or alone, which can be especially important during difficult times. For example, if we are facing a personal challenge, having a strong support system can provide us with the comfort and encouragement we need to get through it.

Another important aspect of relationships is the positive impact they can have on our mental health. Studies have

shown that people who have strong relationships with others are more likely to have better mental health, less stress,
and lower rates of depression and anxiety. This is because
social connections can provide us with a sense of security, a
safe space to express ourselves, and opportunities to engage
in meaningful activities that bring joy and fulfillment to our
lives.

In addition, having strong relationships with others can also
help us build a more positive outlook on life. When we have
people in our lives who care about us and support us, we are
more likely to feel confident, valued, and appreciated. This,
in turn, can help us develop a more optimistic attitude, even
when life throws us curveballs.

It's also important to note that building strong relationships
takes time and effort. Whether it's making time for regular
phone calls, planning activities, or simply being there for
one another, it's crucial that we actively engage in the relationships we have with those closest to us.

One way to build stronger relationships is by practicing
mindful communication. This means being present in the
moment, listening attentively, and expressing ourselves in a

way that is honest, open, and respectful. When we communicate mindfully, we are more likely to build trust and understanding with those around us, which can deepen our connections and foster a more positive outlook on life.

In conclusion, strong relationships with friends and family play a crucial role in our overall well-being and happiness. They provide us with a sense of connectedness, support, and comfort, and can help us cultivate and maintain an optimistic outlook on life. By making an effort to engage in meaningful activities, communicate mindfully, and build trust and understanding with those closest to us, we can reap the numerous benefits of having strong relationships with friends and family.

29: Overcoming Self-Doubt and Building Self-Confidence

Self-doubt can be one of the biggest hindrances to living a life full of optimism and confidence. It can prevent you from pursuing your dreams and reaching your full potential. But with the right mindset and techniques, it is possible to overcome self-doubt and build self-confidence. In this chapter, we will explore the causes of self-doubt and some of the strategies you can use to conquer it.

Self-doubt often stems from negative thoughts and beliefs about yourself. These thoughts can come from past experiences, criticisms from others, or simply from a lack of self-awareness. Some common causes of self-doubt include:

– Perfectionism: Setting unrealistic expectations for yourself can lead to feelings of self-doubt when you can't meet those expectations.

– Comparison: Comparing yourself to others can lead to feelings of inadequacy and self-doubt.

– Fear of failure: The fear of not succeeding can lead to self-doubt and prevent you from taking action.

29: OVERCOMING SELF-DOUBT AND BUILDING SELF-CONFIDENCE

– Low self-esteem: If you don't feel good about yourself, you are more likely to doubt your abilities and decisions.

To overcome self-doubt, it's important to start by identifying the thoughts and beliefs that are causing it. Once you have identified these negative thoughts, you can challenge them by asking yourself if they are really true. This will help you to reframe your thoughts in a more positive light and develop a healthier perspective.

In addition to reframing your thoughts, there are other strategies you can use to build self-confidence and overcome self-doubt. These include:

– Setting realistic goals: By setting achievable goals, you can build your confidence as you make progress and achieve them.

– Surrounding yourself with positive people: Surrounding yourself with supportive and positive people can help boost your self-confidence.

– Practicing self-compassion: Treating yourself with kindness and understanding can help you overcome feelings of

29: OVERCOMING SELF-DOUBT AND BUILDING SELF-CONFIDENCE

self-doubt and build self-confidence.

– Facing your fears: Confronting your fears can help you overcome self-doubt and build self-confidence.

– Celebrating your successes: Celebrating your successes, no matter how small, can help boost your self-confidence and overcome self-doubt.

Finally, it's important to remember that building self-confidence is a journey and not a destination. It takes time and practice to overcome self-doubt, but with persistence and the right mindset, it's possible to achieve. By adopting an optimistic attitude, you can cultivate the self-confidence you need to reach your full potential and live a life filled with joy and success.

In conclusion, overcoming self-doubt and building self-confidence is a critical component of living a life full of optimism and confidence. By identifying the causes of self-doubt, reframing negative thoughts, and practicing self-compassion and other strategies, you can overcome self-doubt and build self-confidence. Remember, building self-confidence takes time and practice, but with persistence and the right mindset, you can achieve it and live a life filled with joy, success, and unshakable confidence.

30: The Power of Acceptance and Letting Go of Perfectionism

Perfectionism is a common problem that affects many people, and it can have a profound impact on our lives. It can cause us to feel overwhelmed and stressed, leading us to avoid taking risks or pursuing our dreams. At the same time, it can also lead to feelings of self-doubt and low self-esteem. However, the good news is that there is a way to overcome these negative effects and find a more positive and fulfilling life. The key is to learn how to accept and let go of perfectionism.

One of the first steps in letting go of perfectionism is to become more aware of it. This means recognizing when you are being overly critical or perfectionistic in your thoughts, and learning to see these patterns for what they are. By understanding what triggers your perfectionism, you can begin to change your behavior and find a more positive outlook.

One effective way to overcome perfectionism is through mindfulness. Mindfulness is the practice of being present in the moment and focusing on your thoughts and feelings without judgment. By becoming more mindful, you can learn to let go of your perfectionistic thoughts and focus on what is truly important to you. This can help you to gain a new perspective on life and to find a greater sense of peace and happiness.

Another important step in overcoming perfectionism is to learn to accept and embrace your imperfections. This means embracing your flaws and imperfections, and recognizing that they are a natural part of who you are. By accepting yourself, you can begin to see that your imperfections do not define you, and that you are worthy of love and respect just as you are.

One of the most powerful ways to build self-confidence and let go of perfectionism is to practice self-compassion. Self-compassion is the act of being kind and understanding towards yourself, and recognizing that everyone makes mistakes and has flaws. By practicing self-compassion, you can learn to accept and embrace your imperfections, and find a greater sense of confidence and self-esteem.

In conclusion, the power of acceptance and letting go of perfectionism is immense. By becoming more aware of your perfectionistic tendencies, learning to be mindful, accepting yourself and your imperfections, and practicing self-compassion, you can find a greater sense of peace and happiness, and be well on your way to a more confident and optimistic life.

31: The Importance of Embracing Failure as a Path to Growth

Embracing failure as a path to growth is a key component of an optimistic mindset. Many people struggle with perfectionism, the belief that they must always succeed and never make mistakes. While this drive to excel can be a positive motivator, it can also lead to feelings of anxiety, stress, and low self-esteem when things don't go as planned.

Optimists, on the other hand, embrace failure as an opportunity for growth. They understand that setbacks and mistakes are inevitable and that they can learn from them. Instead of feeling defeated, they view failure as a stepping stone on their path to success. By embracing failure, optimists are able to remain confident, even in the face of adversity.

One of the benefits of embracing failure is that it allows us to take risks. When we view failure as a path to growth, we are more likely to try new things and push beyond our comfort zone. This is because we are not as concerned about the outcome and are more focused on the learning and growth that can come from the experience.

31: THE IMPORTANCE OF EMBRACING FAILURE AS A PATH TO GROWTH

Additionally, embracing failure helps us to build resilience. When we face challenges and setbacks, it can be tempting to give up and throw in the towel. However, by viewing failure as an opportunity to learn and grow, we are better able to bounce back and continue on our journey. This resilience is key to achieving success in both our personal and professional lives.

Another benefit of embracing failure is that it helps us to develop a growth mindset. A growth mindset is the belief that our abilities and talents can be developed through hard work and perseverance. When we view failure as a path to growth, we are more likely to see challenges as opportunities to improve and develop our skills.

In conclusion, embracing failure as a path to growth is an essential component of an optimistic mindset. By embracing failure, we are better able to take risks, build resilience, and develop a growth mindset, all of which are key to achieving success and finding joy in life. Whether we are pursuing our personal or professional goals, it is important to embrace failure as a path to growth and to never give up on our dreams.

32: The Benefits of Learning from Setbacks and Moving Forward

Introduction

Life is full of ups and downs, and it can be difficult to maintain a positive outlook when we face challenges and setbacks. However, it is during these moments that our optimism is put to the test. A key aspect of being optimistic is the ability to learn from our mistakes and use them as opportunities for growth and development. In this chapter, we will explore the benefits of learning from setbacks and moving forward with a positive attitude.

The Benefits of Failure

One of the most important aspects of embracing failure is learning to see it as an opportunity for growth. Too often, we see failure as a negative outcome, but in reality, it is one of the most valuable experiences we can have. When we fail, we are given the chance to examine what went wrong and make changes to improve for the future. This can lead to increased knowledge, skills, and wisdom that we can carry forward into future endeavors.

32: THE BENEFITS OF LEARNING FROM SETBACKS AND MOVING FORWARD

In addition, failure can be a powerful motivator. When we experience a setback, it can be difficult to maintain a positive outlook, but it can also push us to work even harder and be more determined to succeed. This can lead to increased resilience and a stronger sense of self-efficacy, or the belief that we can succeed despite obstacles and setbacks.

Moving Forward with Optimism

When we learn from our failures and setbacks, it is important to focus on moving forward with an optimistic attitude. This means shifting our perspective from dwelling on what went wrong to looking for new opportunities and solutions. By focusing on what we can learn and what we can do differently, we can begin to see setbacks as stepping stones on the path to success.

In addition, focusing on what we can control can help us maintain a positive outlook. Instead of worrying about things that are beyond our control, we can focus on the things that we can change and the steps we can take to improve our situation. This can help us feel more in control and more confident in our ability to succeed.

32: THE BENEFITS OF LEARNING FROM SETBACKS AND MOVING FORWARD

Building Resilience

Learning from setbacks and moving forward with an optimistic attitude can also help us build resilience, which is the ability to bounce back from challenges and adversity. Resilience is a critical component of success, as it allows us to maintain a positive outlook and continue pursuing our goals even when things get tough.

There are several strategies that can help us build resilience, including:

– Focusing on the positive: Instead of dwelling on the negative, try to focus on the positive aspects of your situation and what you can be grateful for.

– Practicing self-care: Taking care of yourself is essential for maintaining a positive outlook, so be sure to prioritize self-care activities like exercise, mindfulness, and spending time with loved ones.

– Surrounding yourself with positive people: Surrounding yourself with people who support and encourage you can help you maintain a positive outlook and continue pursuing your goals.

– Reframing setbacks as opportunities for growth: Instead of seeing setbacks as failures, try to see them as opportunities for growth and learning.

Conclusion

Learning from setbacks and moving forward with an optimistic attitude is a critical component of success. By embracing failure as an opportunity for growth, focusing on what we can control, and building resilience, we can maintain a positive outlook and continue pursuing our goals, even when things get tough. With time and practice, you will find that setbacks and failures become less daunting, and you will be able to approach challenges with a sense of optimism and confidence that will help you achieve your goals and live the life you want.

33: The Power of Perseverance and Determination

As the saying goes, "if at first you don't succeed, try, try again." Perseverance and determination are two critical components of optimism, as they help you to overcome obstacles and keep moving forward even when things seem difficult or impossible. In this chapter, we'll explore the benefits of perseverance and determination, and how they can help you to cultivate an optimistic outlook, find joy, and achieve success.

Perseverance is the quality of continuing to work hard towards a goal, despite facing difficulties and setbacks. It's about having the inner strength and resilience to keep pushing forward, even when things don't go as planned. When you're faced with challenges, it can be easy to give up and feel defeated. However, having perseverance means that you have the persistence and drive to keep trying until you reach your goal.

Determination, on the other hand, is the quality of being resolved to achieve a goal, no matter what obstacles you face. It's about having the will and motivation to succeed, even when things are tough. When you're determined, you don't let setbacks discourage you or hold you back. Instead, you use them as opportunities to learn and grow, and to become even stronger and more determined in your pursuit of success.

Together, perseverance and determination can be a powerful combination. When you have both qualities, you have the ability to face adversity with confidence, and to keep moving forward, no matter what. You can overcome any obstacle that comes your way, and you can find joy and success, even in the most challenging of circumstances.

So, how can you cultivate perseverance and determination in your own life? Here are some tips to get you started:

– Set specific and achievable goals. When you have clear, defined goals, it's easier to stay motivated and determined to achieve them. Make sure your goals are specific, measurable, and attainable, and write them down so you can visualize them and stay focused.

– Stay positive and focus on the good. When you're faced with setbacks or obstacles, it can be tempting to focus on the negative. However, focusing on the good and finding the silver lining in difficult situations can help you to maintain a positive attitude and keep moving forward.

– Surround yourself with positive people. Being surrounded by positive, supportive people can help you to stay motivated and inspired. Find friends, family members, or a support group who will encourage you and help you to stay optimistic and determined, even when things are tough.

– Celebrate small wins. Celebrating your successes, no matter how small they may be, can help to build your confidence and keep you motivated. Recognize and reward yourself for your achievements, and use these small wins to build momentum and keep moving forward.

– Practice self-care and self-compassion. Taking care of yourself is essential to maintaining your perseverance and determination. Make sure you're getting enough sleep, eating well, and engaging in activities that bring you joy and relaxation. Additionally, be kind and compassionate to yourself, and don't be too hard on yourself when things don't go as planned.

Perseverance and determination are qualities that can be

developed and strengthened over time. By following these tips and by practicing optimism, you can cultivate these qualities and transform your life with unshakable confidence. When you have perseverance and determination, you have the power to overcome adversity, find joy, and achieve success, no matter what. So, start developing these qualities today, and watch as your life transforms for the better.

34: Finding Inner Peace and Accepting Yourself for Who You Are

In order to lead a life filled with joy, happiness, and confidence, it is important to embrace and accept yourself for who you are. Inner peace is a state of mind that can help you overcome adversity and achieve success, as well as provide a sense of calm and stability in your daily life. In order to cultivate this inner peace, it is necessary to let go of negative self-talk, criticism, and the need for perfectionism.

One of the main benefits of inner peace is the ability to reduce stress and anxiety. When you are at peace with yourself and your life, you are less likely to become overwhelmed by negative thoughts and feelings, and more likely to approach challenges with a calm and optimistic mindset. This can help you manage difficult situations more effectively and achieve your goals with greater ease.

Another key benefit of inner peace is improved self-esteem and confidence. When you accept yourself for who you are and embrace your imperfections, you are less likely to compare yourself to others and feel inadequate. Instead, you are more likely to believe in yourself and your abilities, which can help you approach life with a positive and confident attitude.

To cultivate inner peace and acceptance, there are several strategies you can adopt:

– Mindfulness meditation: This practice involves focusing your attention on the present moment and letting go of negative thoughts and worries. It is a powerful tool for reducing stress and anxiety, as well as improving self-awareness and inner peace.

– Positive self-talk: Pay attention to the language you use when speaking to yourself, and make an effort to replace negative self-talk with positive affirmations. Celebrate your accomplishments and embrace your strengths, rather than dwelling on your shortcomings.

– Gratitude: Practice gratitude by focusing on the things in your life that you are thankful for, such as your health, your family, and your friends. This can help you shift your focus from negative thoughts to positive ones and cultivate a sense of inner peace.

– Surround yourself with positive influences: Seek out

people who support and uplift you, and distance yourself from those who bring you down. A positive and supportive social network can help you maintain a positive outlook and embrace yourself for who you are.

– Engage in activities that bring you joy: Whether it is reading a book, playing a sport, or spending time with loved ones, make time for activities that make you happy and bring you a sense of peace.

By embracing yourself for who you are, practicing mindfulness, and cultivating a positive outlook, you can achieve inner peace and feel more confident, optimistic, and resilient in the face of adversity. Remember, self-acceptance is a journey, not a destination, so be patient and kind to yourself along the way. With time, patience, and practice, you can cultivate inner peace and find joy and happiness in your life.

35: The Importance of Celebrating Your Wins and Acknowledging Your Accomplishments

As human beings, we often focus so much on what we haven't accomplished or the things we still need to improve upon that we forget to take a step back and celebrate the wins and accomplishments we've already achieved. This can be especially true for those who possess an optimistic mindset, as they are always striving to do better and make positive changes in their lives. However, it's important to remember that acknowledging and celebrating your wins and accomplishments is an essential part of maintaining an optimistic outlook.

When we celebrate our wins, it not only helps us to feel good about ourselves, but it also reinforces the idea that we are capable of success. This can build our confidence and encourage us to keep working towards our goals, as we have proof that we have already achieved great things. When we ignore our wins or downplay their significance, we are sending a message to our subconscious that our accomplishments aren't valuable or worth recognizing, which can lead to feelings of self-doubt and a lack of confidence.

35: THE IMPORTANCE OF CELEBRATING YOUR WINS AND ACKNOWLEDGING YOUR ACCOMPLISHMENTS

It's important to note that celebrating your wins doesn't mean you should be arrogant or boastful. It simply means taking a moment to acknowledge what you've accomplished and to feel proud of yourself. This can be as simple as writing down your wins in a journal, sharing them with a friend or loved one, or simply taking a moment to reflect on them and feel grateful for what you've achieved.

In addition to celebrating your own wins, it's also important to acknowledge the accomplishments of those around you. This can be done through simple acts of kindness, such as complimenting a friend on a recent accomplishment or offering support and encouragement to someone who is working towards a goal. By recognizing the achievements of others, we help to create a positive and supportive environment, which can have a significant impact on our own outlook and confidence.

In conclusion, celebrating your wins and acknowledging your accomplishments is a crucial part of maintaining an optimistic attitude. It helps to reinforce the idea that we are capable of success, boost our confidence, and create a positive and supportive environment. So, make sure to take a

35: THE IMPORTANCE OF CELEBRATING YOUR WINS AND ACKNOWLEDGING YOUR ACCOMPLISHMENTS

moment to celebrate your wins and acknowledge the accomplishments of those around you. You'll be amazed at the positive impact it can have on your outlook and overall well-being.

36: Conclusion: Embracing the Power of Optimism for a Better Life

In this book, we have explored the many benefits of embracing an optimistic outlook and how it can transform your life. From building self-confidence and improving relationships, to finding inner peace and experiencing greater success, optimism has the power to bring about positive change in all areas of your life.

The key to unlocking the power of optimism is to practice it every day. This means focusing on the positive aspects of your life and experiences, instead of dwelling on the negative. It also means embracing a growth mindset, viewing failures and setbacks as opportunities for growth and learning, rather than as insurmountable obstacles.

One of the most important aspects of building an optimistic outlook is to cultivate positive self-talk. This means speaking kindly to yourself and acknowledging your strengths, instead of focusing on your weaknesses. It also means being mindful of the words you use when communicating with others, avoiding negative language and seeking to build meaningful connections.

Another crucial component of optimism is giving back and helping others. By focusing on the needs of others, you can broaden your perspective, develop a greater sense of empathy, and feel a deep sense of purpose and fulfillment.

In conclusion, embracing an optimistic outlook is not just about feeling good, it is about creating a better life for yourself and those around you. By committing to a daily practice of optimism, you can build unshakable confidence, overcome adversity, and achieve greater success and happiness in all areas of your life. So take a step forward today, and embrace the power of optimism. Your future self will thank you.

In conclusion, optimism is a powerful tool that can be harnessed to transform your life and help you overcome adversity and achieve success. By developing an optimistic outlook and embracing a positive mindset, you can find joy and happiness in your daily life, build strong relationships with loved ones, and overcome self-doubt and fear. Through mindful communication and self-reflection, you can cultivate self-confidence and develop a healthy relationship with yourself, while learning to accept and embrace your failures as opportunities for growth. By persevering and embracing the power of determination, you can overcome setbacks and achieve your goals, while finding inner peace and embracing who you are.

The key to unlocking the full potential of optimism is to actively cultivate and nurture it in your daily life. Whether through mindfulness practices, positive self-talk, or celebrating your successes and accomplishments, it is important to focus on the things that bring joy and positivity into your life, and to let go of perfectionism and the need for control. With practice and dedication, you can develop an unshakable confidence and an unwavering belief in yourself and your ability to succeed, no matter what obstacles may lie ahead.

Remember, the power of optimism is within you, and it is up to you to harness it and use it to transform your life. By following the principles outlined in this book and embracing the power of positive thinking, you can unlock the full potential of optimism and achieve a life filled with joy, confidence, and success. So go forth and embrace the power of

36: CONCLUSION: EMBRACING THE POWER OF OP-TIMISM FOR A BETTER LIFE

optimism, and let your life be transformed forever.

Thank You

As we reach the end of this book, I want to say thanks for reading this book.

I want to get this information out to as many people as possible. If you found this book helpful, I would greatly appreciate you leaving me a review. This helps others find the book as well.

Disclaimer

This document is geared towards providing exact and reliable information in regards to the topic and issue covered. The publication is sold on the idea that the publisher is not required to render an accounting, officially permitted, or otherwise, qualified services. If advice is necessary, legal, financial, medical or professional, a practiced individual in the profession should be ordered.

This information is not presented by a financial or medical practitioner and is for entertainment, educational and informational purposes only. The content is not intended as a substitute for professional medical advice, diagnosis, or treatment. Always seek the advice of your physician or other qualified health care provider with any questions you may have regarding a medical condition. Never disregard professional medical advice or delay in seeking it because of something you have read.

The information provided herein is stated to be truthful and consistent, in that any liability, in terms of inattention or otherwise, by any usage or abuse of any policies, processes, or directions contained within is the solitary and utter responsibility of the recipient reader. Under no circumstances

DISCLAIMER

will any legal responsibility or blame be held against the publisher for any reparation, damages, or monetary loss due to the information herein, either directly or indirectly.